Between Frames

BETWEEN FRAMES

POEMS & PHOTOGRAPHS
MARK HILLRINGHOUSE

SERVING HOUSE BOOKS

Between Frames

Copyright © 2012 Mark Hillringhouse

All rights reserved

No part of this book may be used or reproduced in any manner whatsoever without the prior written permission of the copyright holder except for brief quotations in critical articles or reviews.

ISBN: 978-0-9838289-8-3

Author photograph by Chris Lovi

Serving House Books logo by Barry Lereng Wilmont

Published by Serving House Books, LLC

Copenhagen, Denmark, and Florham Park, NJ

www.servinghousebooks.com

First Serving House Books Edition 2012

For Linda, who makes the journey possible

"Photographers deal in things which are continually vanishing, and when they have vanished there is no contrivance on earth which can make them come back again."

—Henri Cartier-Bresson

Paterson, Great Falls

Moisture / 16
Orpheus / 18
My Right Ear / 20
Penn Station / 22
Ford Galaxy / 24
Pancakes / 26
Tomato Soup / 228
Le Balcon / 30
Guilt Shop / 32
To a Buick Skylark / 34
Here / 38
Just Before Dark / 40
June 21st / 42
At the Arlington Diner / 44
Ice Cream / 46
On First Looking in Kleinzahler's
   "On First Looking into Joseph Cornell's Diaries" / 48
Memorial Day / 50
At the Ballgame / 54
Throwing Out the Letter "G" / 56
The Mystery and Melancholy of a Street / 58
Living Next Door to Yourself / 60
In Paterson / 64
Mill Street / 66
Dear Walt / 68
Driving Through Paterson / 70
Route 80 / 72
Route 46 / 74
Woolworth's / 76
Diner / 78
Afterimages / 83

Mark Hillringhouse's "Universe of light"

*Between Frames i*s a hard book to put down. It is hard to put down because it is so slender—so slender and so simple and so precise and so full of the mystery of simple everyday things, everyday experiences, that you can lose yourself for hours in it, in the single image of a photograph, in the hypnotic light and shadow, in a single line or image of a poem.

Mark Hillringhouse's photographs are poems, his poems are photographs—of a dead father ("Moisture"), of a dead mother's "gold dress she wore to my wedding," of "the whispered voices/of children dreaming / inside my skull" ("My Right Ear"), of children running to catch fireflies—"how impossible it is to catch light" ("Ford Galaxy"), which on the opposite page faces a photograph breathtaking in its light-capturing darkness.

Or consider the hypnotizing simplicity of a close-up: cup, saucer, spoon, and their shadow, nothing else—this is reality, you understand, this object, these objects you see everyday but never really see until they are captured in an image on a page so stunningly precise that you finally *see* it in all its simplicity and mystery. Simple and mysterious as the exquisite simplicity and exquisite complexity of the multitude of wrinkles of a slept-in unmade bed, beautiful and dingy as life itself.

I first came to Mark Hillringhouse's photographs at a presentation he made one day of the pictures he had taken of the New York Poets he hung around with and photographed in the '70s and '80s – Ashbery, Baraka, Berrigan, Merwin, Kenneth Koch, Allen Ginsberg, Gregory Corso, Philip Whalen, Ron Padgett, Anne Waldman, Gerald Stern, Jack Gilbert, C. K. Williams, Linda Gregg, and many others. I was fascinated by what he could capture in black-and-white portraits of poets that had the precision of light and shadow of poems in themselves. A couple of years later I remembered the quality of those pictures when I wanted a photograph of the Queensboro Bridge on the cover of a book of essays I was doing with New American Press. I wanted a photograph moving in toward New York City from the east side of the East River that gave the impression of looking back across the whole continent of the U.S.A., but first you have to get through Manhattan and all of its walls. Because a writer has all these tens of thousands of words at his disposal, he really thinks that a picture can say everything he wants it to.

So I wrote to Mark Hillringhouse to ask if he had something like that, and he didn't, but he went on a safari to Queens to take one.

"I chose the quietest day of the year," he said. "Super Bowl Sunday at the end of February. It was early morning and the drug dealers were still in bed. The streets were empty and there were so few cars that I was even able to stop in the middle of the bridge heading into Manhattan and get out to take a photograph. Not a cop in sight. I made four or five crossings, driving back and forth over the bridge and circling around. I finally found my approach on the Queens side in a park along the East River. The light was amazing. Those long, early morning, eastern shadows across Manhattan. It was a magical moment."

And it was, I think, a magical cover for my book (*Riding the Dog: A Look Back at America,* 2008). He did it again for my next book with New American Press, with his photograph of a slept-in bed (*Last Night My Bed a Boat of Whiskey Going Down,* 2010), and it looks like he will do it again with a cover for my forthcoming story collection of an incredibly evocative photograph (also in this book, on page 39) of a writing desk and chair and radiator and a window with its curtain askew. That photograph, in fact, is a picture of the writing desk of Gerald Stern (Poet Laureate of New Jersey, 2000-2002).

It is all about light and shadow, light and darkness, whether it is a photograph or a poem about a "city that has no more memory of itself / than a river has of rain" and about "an emptied storefront, rays of sunlight poking in / to finger the dusty hollowness of barren shelves" ("Woolworth's"). The eye of a fine poet is like the eye of a master photographer—in a diner, it sees "tin ashtrays…stacked and bent inside each other next to ketchup bottles / Lined up like pints of blood" and "the universe of light in the chrome reflection off / Napkin dispensers," reminding over a cup of 2 a.m. coffee "that it is always better here behind the plate glass / In the light than outside traveling through the darkness" ("Diner").

I could go on and on about these photographs which are poems and these poems which are photographs, but there is really no reason for me to try to describe in *my* words what Mark Hillringhouse has already done better with *his* words and *his* magical crafting of light and shadow. He brings forth the mystery and the complex simplicity of whatever he looks upon and casts into art—whether it is the eerie light of an empty diner, the harsh sweet hourly rental of a motel vacancy on Route 46, a highway, a Laundromat, a crystal doorknob, a bridge, a road, or just a jagged shadow down a flight of concrete stairs, or a poem about Walt Whitman puzzling over a piece of plastic ("It has nothing to return to. / It will not feed the grass."), and a photograph of a fat old cat sitting in an armchair and daring you with its insolent angry puss to try to take that chair—you realize it will fight you hard because that chair is all it has. Wait a sec—you think you recognize that cat. In fact, you think it was Ted Berrigan's cat, named Wystan after W. H. Auden, and the tin box where Berrigan kept his poetry postcards is on the floor by the chair in Berrigan's apartment on St. Mark's Place. And the expression on the face of that cat, on the face of Wystan, is saying, *Berrigan is dead and you won't get this chair without a fight*.

But you have your own chair and a good book, and you will have many hours of amazement and mystery with this book—because it is so slender and so precise that you will never want to put it down.

—Thomas E. Kennedy, Author of *The Copenhagen Quartet*

Door Knob

MOISTURE

I can still hear the phone ring
then silence, then the phone again.
I'm up and out of bed at 5 am, my brother
on the other end, "Dad passed away."

I can still see my brother
in the lobby waiting for me.
I can still see my father's body:
pale, gray, wooden.

It's a strange kind of birth
being born out of the body,
that cold, eerie stillness—

I am snowed in; it snowed all night,
snowed all morning, all day into evening.

My father made it snow,
his spirit in the upper atmosphere
got swept up in a storm.

There is a Hopi legend
that the spirit returns as moisture,
and now he's snowing all around me,

his spirit melting into the cold air,
melting into the earth,
in snowflakes melting into streams,
melting into underground rivers.

Winter Fog

ORPHEUS

I say goodbye to each item
cleaning out my mother's apartment—
like stations of the cross,
I pause where my father's L-A-Z Boy
sat in the corner of the living room,
where he'd jump up to greet me
whenever I walked in.
I stand at the doorway to my old bedroom
where I spent my days
sleeping till noon, smoking cigarettes,
staying up all night reading.
I stop at the dining room,
and look at the worn out rug and chairs
from years of sitting eating
while no one talked,
or ever said a prayer.
I switch off the kitchen light
that was always on.
I take whatever I can carry:
a blue china bowl, some cups,
some antique pewter—
I fill garbage bags with all her clothes:
the gold dress she wore to my wedding
in the back of her closet
hiding like some frightened bird
where she hid her bottles.
I was frightened of her back then,
she demanded so much.
My worst fear was being stuck
after dad died, and then her stroke,
the car accident, taking care of her
for five years until she gave up
and I gave so little.
I grab the dress before it falls
and fold it on top
of all her clothes to give away.
The last thing to go—her bed,
too big for the elevator
and the two Mexicans I hire
to remove furniture speak no English.
I tell them that they can get it through
the exit to the fire escape
gesturing with my hands
and I watch as they drag its carcass out
and I step out and let the front door bang,
descend three flights of marble steps,
one hand on the iron balustrade,
and make my getaway
not looking back
for fear of what I left behind
seeing my dead father's name
for the last time taped above the bell.
And as the Mexicans dangle
the mattress from the third floor
fire escape, I look and catch
the last image of my mother—
her urine stains outlining where her body lay,
as they let go and drop her mattress
to the ground;
I see the yellow outline of her head, torso,
arms and legs,
like the Shroud of Turin, as it slowly falls,
and I turn back
trying not to think and trying not to cry
leaving that apartment
as if no one ever lived there
putting the car in gear and driving away.

Stairwell

My Right Ear

There are days
when I seem to hear nothing
but the voices of children
drowning in a well.

From my bed at night
I could hear
my mother sob
as my father yelled
and slammed the door.

In the damp, north corner
of my room
on the lower bunk,
my good ear buried in the pillow,
the muffled voices,

like water
inside my skull
from a punctured eardrum
the doctors mistreated
with peroxide and sulfur.
But nothing could take away the pain,

and hearing late at night
my father stumble in,
fumbling with his keys,
and ready to break down the door,
then passing out
until I heard him snore.

I can still hear
the terrors of waking
from the cold sadness of that house:
the distal pulse of blood
like the whispered voices
of children drowning
inside my skull.

Unmade Bed

Penn Station

One day you're out playing in the yard,
then someone hits a ball that sails clear out
over the fence and gets lost in the weeds
and the game is over.
Or the boys are chasing the girls down a hill
and it's sunny and the grass is wild and
someone starts rolling and the day spreads out
around the sky and the earth becomes dizzy.
Then the bell rings and you're called back
from recess and the next thing you know
you're suited up in some weird kind of army,
a leather valise in one hand, the hard facts of life
in the other, a train schedule in your pocket.
And everyone you've ever played with
is out marching or waiting in line somewhere,
all except me, as I sit this one out
to watch the starched and ironed gray parade
because I'm still out there rolling in the grass,
still feeling dizzy, still reeling from holding onto
the earth, still searching in the weeds.

Lackawanna Station, Hoboken

Ford Galaxy

Your father pulls in the driveway
in a brand new Ford.
Your mother's long, red hair
is tied back under a white, silk kerchief.
She is almost smiling in a sort of sneer
about her miserable life,
in a house with two kids.
And you can almost see the future
stretching out to better days
in chrome and Vinyl.
The fireflies rise off the grass,
the days are young, your life will never end.
The neighborhood kids run hoping to catch
enough green light to fill a glass.
As you run down the dark lawn
how impossible it is
to gather light.
And you
begin to disappear
where evening rises out of the ground,
in back of the house, and inside your room,
where darkness never ends.

Backyard July

Pancakes

Roused from sleep
and standing in pajamas
my father made us pancakes:
"How many you kids want?"
My brother fighting for the first order,
"Ten, stacked and smeared with butter."
Drowning them in Aunt Jemima's,
milk, eggs and batter splattered everywhere.
It's the only time I ever saw him
in the kitchen all those years at home—
men in my family never learned to cook,
the penalty for our sins was church:
two hours on a hardwood pew
in wool jacket, starched shirt and knotted tie.
I lost myself in the rafters,
in the light outside pouring through
the stained glass windows,
in the organ music and the choir,
in hymns and prayers I never understood.
All offerings went to the Father.
I thought about my own father
staying home to watch the ball games
and made up my own benedictions
in silence in the blood of Christ,
an open wound we bathed in:
forgiveness for the taste of flesh
left in our mouths like bread.

Church Ceiling

Tomato Soup

I know it's good for me,
plain soup out of a tin can.
And now I'm learning to avoid all the excess,
to hunt for bargains in the afternoon,
to change the oil on the old car,
to wear the same shirt two days in a row.
I follow the simple directions:
add one can of water,
heat and stir.
If my own life had directions,
I could live forever
slowly working my way from the cool edges
to the hot center with my spoon.
I'd learn from the mistakes
my grandmother taught my mother,
I'd learn that nothing can ease the pain in my heart.
I know Whitman had a bowl for lunch
before he died. Carloads of Jersey tomatoes
coming in to the steaming vats
on the rails to Camden.
Maybe I'll clean out the pot,
write letters, read, take a nap,
and when I wake go stand outside
and ladle in a bowlful of its darkness
with my hands.

Cup, Spoon, & Saucer

LE BALCON

I sat as high and as far back
as I could go getting nowhere
with a girl from high school.

My fantasies reeled out
in fondled breasts
in the smell of perfumed hair
and buttered popcorn.

O toi tous mes plaisirs, O toi tous mes devoirs

Huddled in a dim and musty movie house
my head filled with the projector's cricket chirps
as the light flickered.

I smoked cigarettes...

O douceur! O poison!

and tried to impress
my grasp of Baudelaire
and high school French
upon her.

But what did I know
of "le charme des soirs"
or "les soleils rajeunis."
I was just a kid
cutting class
to see French films
in the back of the balcony

waiting for the curtains to crack
open for the sky to turn black,
for the dark to surround me
with a girl from Hackensack.

Fabian Theater, Paterson

GUILT SHOP

(from misreading a road sign that said
"Quilt Shop")

All there in one place,
everything you've ever felt bad about
losing or breaking
next to those items
you should have gotten
but forgot—
Like the time you forgot
your wife's birthday,
or your brother's graduation,
or your best friend's wedding.
On the wall
is the half-hearted,
last minute, cheap substitute
for a gift you gave your mother
one Mother's Day.
You still remember
how you hated to give her anything.
And over by the door
is the chair you smashed
for something you no longer care about.
All the things
you ever hurled in a fit of rage
and had to sweep up
are for sale here.

Piece by piece,
you pick them up again
and fondle the torn photographs
and letters you ripped apart,
all symbols of your life:
The rock you threw at your brother
is displayed on the counter.
The money you stole
is in the cash register
in an envelope with your name,
along with the loan you never repaid.
The clocks with minutes of your life ticking out,
all the time you wasted,
is recorded here:
the nights you got drunk,
the women you walked out on,
the phone calls you promised to make,
the poems you would write—
everything you ever gave up,
everyone you ever rejected,
everything you ever felt bad about,
or destroyed in a fit of rage
is for sale here.

Colt Mill Ruins

To a Buick Skylark

Hail to thee O first car!
my father's beat up Buick,
the car I'd fall asleep in
on long drives home.

And here's to getting laid
on the back seat,
the windows steamed,
and a cop banging on the windshield.

Ugly as it was I loved that car,
even now as I drive past places
I remember growing up.
I feel a sense of gladness
knowing how it felt to spin out,
knowing how my life would go off course,
knowing that what I needed
had nothing to do with cars,
or spinning out,
or getting laid.

'53 Buick

Radiator

HERE

    for Gerald Stern

Here is where you will always be,
in this never ending now,
even if you use the future,
or the past,
a trick of language to escape
to a place that doesn't exist.
You are forever leaning in your chair,
your head tilted like the prow of a ship,
looking out the window
waiting for the next moment
to crash over you
in dark waves
drowning the warm animal
breathing by your side.

Gerald Stern's Study, Lambertville, NJ

JUST BEFORE DARK

    for George Tice

I love the way faces seem to glow at dusk.
Someone said a touch of setting sun adds warmth,
and someone else thought to speak of summer moonlight on the grass,
but I knew that what I loved was the edge of light,
the sharp-edged shadows falling from the sky,
and the soft-edge shadows rising from the ground,
and that I was riding the bow wake of a long afternoon into evening,
a gift someone said from no one we could name,
the foam behind us hissing in our faces.

Dusk

June 21

How easy it is
to be fooled by the life
in the photograph:
wind-frozen hair, sun
in your eyes, teeth
as white as smiles
cloud more permanent
than either sadness or misgiving.
You learn nothing from fallen angels—
you only know the continual
good life of tan trousers,
the clear liquid image
of water under a blue sky.
You are never alone.
Your arm is around the shoulder
of a friend you left years ago,
raising the dead fish
dripping with blood, heads
almost touching.
You are never out of music,
neither starving or thirsty.
As you stand on a wave,
the brim of your hat is slanted
the way the rest of the afternoon
tilts under the horizon
on the longest day of the year.

Angel Billboard, Vineland, NJ

AT THE ARLINGTON DINER

   (after Malena Morling)

If there is another world,
you can ride there
down the old county road,
past the Sealed Air Corporation,
or pull into Eric's Auto World
and walk down to the river's edge
and sit in the park on the bank
where a woman's body washed up,
or paddle your way with the tide
around the Garfield Bend,
past the Russian cathedral,
past the teddy-bear memorial
for the niece whose uncle drowned her
off the Gregory Avenue Bridge.
And from there you can drift
all the way out to Newark Bay
swirling a little past Belleville,
going under the last iron bridge
with the gatehouse attached to it,
and past the cemetery
and on to the parking lot.
And if you're inclined to,
you can stop at the Arlington Diner
for a slice of "World Famous" cheesecake,
knowing sooner or later
even the names on the gravestones
will wash away,
knowing sooner or later,
the iron bridges will streak with rust
like iron tears,
the way everything wants to tear inside
and wash away into the river.
And I can draw a map on how to get there
writing directions on the back of a placemat
on how not to get lost, while gazing
at my fogged reflection in the cold glass
as if I didn't already think of myself
as a kind of ghost.
And shouldn't every day be a day
of trying to reach another world,
of seeing the gas fires burn off in the distance
over the Linden refineries.
And shouldn't every day
be spent wrapped in clouds
in search of cities that fade into mist.
And aren't all lives strange,
as I dream myself
climbing some dark stairs
to a room above a bar,
or to be holding onto things
and letting go,
as if there was another world.
The waitress, as she waddles by,
startles me wielding a pot of coffee,
as she calls me "hun,"
refills my cup,
and slaps the bill
on the counter.

Arlington Diner

ICE CREAM

This is a poem that has nothing to do with ice cream
It is a poem about how refrigerators will take over the world
It is a poem about how girls come apart in the wind
How the dead love their cats
How old songs can be sung almost anywhere
How everyone loves cold beer and hot dogs
It is a poem about fidgeting, about staring over a cliff
And hearing late at night the needle-like
voice of your mother whir in your ear.

Winter, Great Falls

On First Looking into August Kleinzahler's "On First Looking into Joseph Cornell's Diaries"

Much have I travelled in a Kleinzahler poem,
replete with weather and cafés
and street people doing their thing,
like a girl putting on makeup
and tossing a cigarette
in the early light of a sad, gray spring,
the snow all melted, so close you can hear
parked cars touching
with only enough space for a garbage can,
like a Joseph Cornell box if it were painted
bright blue and someone balanced an egg
on its end and stuck a bird in a cage.
But now I am trying to figure out where to begin,
or what I'm doing in the middle of Kleinzahler's poem
where he has turned on the TV
and Kleinzahler would be good company
if he were around and we could both laugh together,
but I feel like I am almost out of the poem,
just a few lines to go, but they're on a page
all alone like a sonnet divided into couplets
and a five-line quatrain. I don't think
that I will ever be gazing up at some page
lying in bed un-showered in the early afternoon
"like some watcher of the skies"
on a day I only woke to stay in bed,
until I heard Kleinzahler speak loud and bold
and suddenly he's gone
"my special Thursday dream"
to read his new book of poems
now that the landscapers have arrived
with their terrible loud machines.

Main Street, Paterson

Memorial Day

    in memory of Ted Berrigan (1934-1983)

I pull down the selected "So Going Around Cities"
which you signed twice because I bought two copies
and one I gave away but I tore out the page you signed
in the one I gave away and stuck it in the other one you signed
so the torn-out page reads:
"for Mark in Hoboken 13 November 1980
after listening to Jack Kerouac together affectionately, Ted Berrigan,"
and the other reads:
"For Mark with admiration and affection from Ted Berrigan 29 August 1982."
I remember that was in your apartment, 101 Saint Mark's Place,
you on your mattress, shirt off, head on pillow,
lit Chesterfield dangling precariously from lower lip,
ashes falling on your chest, the phone ringing,
Alice in the next room, Anselm and Edmund squirming
as you said, "like eels" in their bunk beds.
I turn to "Memorial Day" your long poem about death,
and you mention the death of poets you love instead of war dead,
an idea you got from Frank O'Hara,
who is very much at the center of your poem,
and I wonder about the structure, the spaces between lines,
the way the lines repeat down the page,
the odd syntax and personal references to people you knew
and loved both living and dead that mattered to you
and how you listed their names
and the way you kept the poem going,
all questions I would ask you now, as I read
realizing I am six years older than you were
the last time I saw you a month before you died
July Fourth nineteen eighty-three when you were only forty-eight
when I thought of you as a father.
I think it was your beard, the long gray hair,
the burden of your life, the weight of all those books

in your head that made you look older than you did,
plus the pills and the cigarettes. And a "New Yorker"
notepad page falls out,
(I used to stick odds and ends inside books for safe keeping)
that reads, "Dear Mark, Found 'em!
the Stevens is yours, too? Best, Vickie"
who was Howard Moss's assistant,
and I remember giving some of your books to Howard,
the poetry editor and another poet I had gotten to know
who liked your work, especially your poem "My Autobiography"
which was a postcard poem that read:
"For Love of Megan I danced all night…"
I thought this was incredible for how deeply personal
your poems are made from talks and visits with friends,
and in the way you talked and kept on talking,
like the time I was visiting and the poet Eileen Myles
stopped in and you said that I should go out with her
even though she was a lesbian,
or the time you introduced me to that asshole
René Ricard at Alice's book party at the Gotham Bookstore
and she got so drunk that she signed her book to me to someone else
and I walked back over to her and handed her the book
and told her to sign it over
which you thought was "terrific"
--your term for what you felt was genuine and real.
And as I look through and turn the pages
my black and white head shot of you falls out,
that soulful look that I tried to capture,
the sad eyes swimming in the bare bulb incandescent light of your room,
the Scotch-taped, horn-rimmed glasses sliding off your nose
magnifying their expression, a photograph that everyone loved
because it revealed your sensitive and fragile ego
that all of us share. Then I find two postcards that you gave me.
I remember sitting in your living room which was rare,
since you were always on your back every time I came to see you.
But this time you were up and you handed me a tin box

with a hundred hand-written postcards
and you told me to choose a couple and I did,
and when I showed you the ones that I chose you said,
"You took all the good ones!"
and so you took those back and handed me these two:
"Christmas in September" which you signed, "for Mark Hillringhouse"
and on the bottom was written in your distinctive handwriting
and in parentheses (after Alice Notley)
and the other postcard was one you wrote about Bernadette Mayer
and on it you had glued an old photograph of Bernadette
at age 16 in a nightgown standing by her bed in her bedroom
with the date "1958" beneath it with the title "St. Bernadette & All That"
—It was a card that you didn't want her to see
and so you gave it to me because you and Bernadette
had had a falling out over some alleged stolen copies of your "Sonnets"
that Bernadette and Lewis Warsh had reprinted
under their United Artists label and bad blood between you
came out in places like the reading I remember that you gave at Saint Mark's
with Bernadette in the audience and you said some words.
And now I have the angry postcard
but you had no way of knowing that Bernadette would later have a stroke
and be paralyzed and unable to write
but this would be years after your death,
but I know that you would have felt sorry for her.
And when I went back recently to where you used to live
to take some photographs, there was a line of tourists
waiting on your stoop to get in the French restaurant
that opened up next door. Hard to believe how trendy
this old neighborhood became in twenty years
and so expensive you could never live here.
And who lives here now that you are gone?
and Alice is in Paris, and Allen is dead
and so many others like Steve and Jim and Michael
and Edwin, Jimmy and Kenneth.
And so I quote your line about friendship:
"Make friends forever and disappear."

Ted Berrigan's Cat, 101 St. Mark's Place

AT THE BALLGAME

    after William Carlos Williams
    Shea Stadium: Mets 7, Giants 3—July 10, 2008

    —for Ken Karol

The scoreboard flashes—Make Noise!
as Wright hits one into the stands,
the fans are up on their feet.
I am on line for a bottle of beer ($8)
In the left field mezzanine.
This is my last time at Shea,
the new stadium, a brick, retro Ebbett's Field,
looms ready to open. I wear
the Mets blue hat with orange NY letters,
my shirt is drenched with sweat.
I came to take photographs
before they tear it down.
The new name is not even a name,
just a corporate logo, some greedy bank—
what does banking have to do with baseball?
There is not one single space
where there isn't an ad,
even the fans are walking billboards,
and around the diamond and the outfield
everything pixilated, video streamed,
shifting color like an electric octopus:
fans' faces, players' faces, box scores,
I am lost, I am dizzy, I am tripping,
I am fluttering like a moth in Times Square,
there's something corporate fascist in the air,
the Star Spangled Banner flies everywhere
marketed into sodas and hotdogs,
into something primitive and tribal,
into something that separates us
from something we fear and hate in each other.

Hinchliffe Stadium, Paterson

Throwing Out the Letter "G"

>In throwing out my old Colliers Encyclopedia, I decided last minute to rescue one volume lying on top of the garbage, the letter "G," and started reading, and I read the whole volume because I wanted to know what I was throwing away…

It seemed a shame to throw away a name like gadolinium—
lustrous rare magnetic metal of the earth,

or the lovely galactosemia, no Greek goddess but a disease
preventing one from becoming too sweet like Galib,

love poet of the Ottomans. Or Evariste Galois, who wrote about the impossibility
of solving the quintic equation.

And who can do without gamboge used to make yellow watercolor,
or who can pass by Gandor, New Foundland,

and we should never forget Garcilaso de la Vega,
poet of the Golden Age, inventor of the rhyming stanza called the lira;

or Garfield, New Jersey, or Charles Julius Guiteau
who killed Garfield,

or Hector de Saint Denys Garneau whose "Regards et Jeux dans l'Espace"
broke new ice in French Canada:

his only subject—death and loneliness.
Too bad he never got to know André Garnerin

who jumped three thousand feet from a balloon with a handmade parachute
not knowing if it would work.

And who would want to forget the garrote, an iron collar tightened with a screw,
or Friedrich Von Gartner who developed the Rundbogenstil derived from the Quattrocento,

or poor Friedrich Gauss who discovered theorems that had already been discovered,
or the gaur, wild ox of the Steppes, or the "Gavotte" a lively peasant dance

where couples bend and sway then fart and hand each other flowers.
Or Ricardo Guiraldes, who celebrated the gaucho in his novel, "Shadows on the Pampas."

Or Guido Guinicelli, father of the dolce stil nuovo, or "sweet new style,"
or the gutta-pucha, hard, brittle and cold when solid, soft when hot, made into balata.

Or Beno Gutenberg discoverer of the boundary between earth's mantle and core,
or Nell Gwynne, King Charles II's mistress, former bad actress known for selling oranges

on the street, last stage appearance—Dryden's "The Conquest of Granada"
king's last words: "Don't let poor Nellie starve!"

Or who would want to ever forget the Japanese painter Gyokudo of the "Nango School"
whose mountain landscapes titled "Two Peaks Embracing Clouds"

Made him take up a life of wandering
in search of the dark, mysterious forces of the letter "G"

Passaic River

THE MYSTERY AND MELANCHOLY OF A STREET

after a photograph I took in Binghamton, NY
that reminded me of de Chirico's painting

Down a long, deserted street,
a kid's shadow falls on the walls
of vacant buildings--
There is danger in his stare,
the fear of strangers,
a kind of burnt umber that I love
in the aftermath of this city,
that deep, red brick burning in the sun,
the hush of cold, dark rivers moving
as he moves past empty rooms,
past rows of warehouse windows,
past rail yards into the fading light
of a lonely, late afternoon
in search of some place to go.

Binghamton, NY

LIVING NEXT DOOR TO YOURSELF

What does he do all day?
You see him once or twice a week
darting from his car to the garage.
You see the second floor light go on
in the corner study. What work does he do
sitting in the corner of his room all night?
Most of the time, the house is quiet,
and you are grateful for the silence.
He doesn't always rake his leaves
or rakes them in the dark;
and he mows his grass at odd hours,
lets it go for weeks. How strange you think,
And you notice
that when he does step outside
he stares up at the sky.
The couple of times you've actually met,
he doesn't talk about the weather or sports,
but talks about how the sunlight slants
in a corner of the yard, and how he wishes
he could capture the way the lonely fat kid
down the end of the block leans
his bicycle against a wall.
You wonder what goes on in that house:
no children, not even a dog,
just books piled in the windows.
And you notice how
the lights never come on,
just the one light up in the study,
his garage falling down,
a blue tarp over the hole in the roof,
a bath towel pinned across the bedroom window,
the garden ruined with weeds,
overgrown, abandoned, let go, wild.

Bicycle

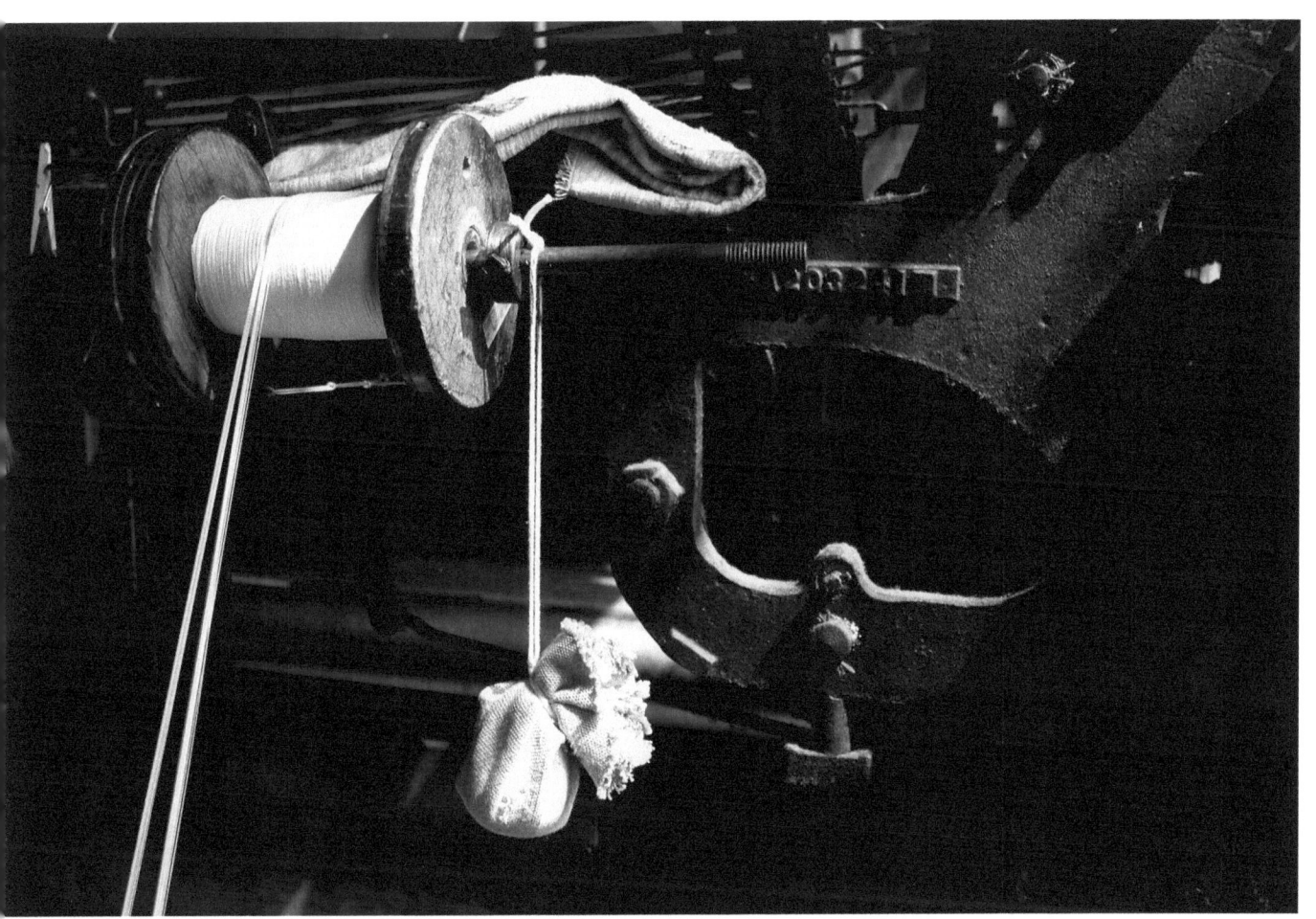

Silk Loom

In Paterson

    in memory of Tommy Greco

Under the giant shadow
of the Broadway Bank
gazing into shop windows,
on the corner of Market and Main,
I feel like one of those sixteenth century
Dutch figures in one of Brueghel's
great paintings.
I wonder if there's a connection to anything
as I stand here with a head full of questions
like who put me in this picture?
I should probably be off fishing,
or finding my place
among the clouds in another river town
of hills and factories.
Questions spill out of my head
like the rivers of my desire,
one happy, one sad to be alone.
And I know there's a meaning to all this
now that you're gone--
even the buildings look tired
and the streets a little sadder,
even as I blend into this background
of weirdos and strangers
who stick their necks out like gargoyles
and shout obscenities from street corners,
even as I watch a homeless man
dressed for winter in the middle of July
dance to the Saint Vitas music in his head,
I enter Woolworth's to buy something,
something I don't need that'll end up
as garbage amid the squalor
on Grand Street,
where a father bends over to kiss his son,
knowing that we all begin and end
pretty much in the same way,
and the difference a little love
makes in our lives,
when I think of you sitting in your chair
by the window
and the sunlight you slept in,
or when you stood behind the bar
and gave us some comfort for our troubles,
when all we talked about
was the boredom around us,
and the jobs we hated,
and the places we called home.

Market Street, Paterson

Mill Street (Essex Mill 1984-1986)

I'm living in Paterson,
a little too much living
and not enough sleep
while people in the office
are plotting to get rid of me
and a woman down the hall
is eating a cupcake.
She believes someone
is always trying to steal
her newspaper,
but I always bring it back.
It is just that the wind whistles
over the cracks and along
the rows of broken chimneys,
and all this is mine
as I walk to the elevator
without opening my eyes
because I don't have any particular center,
because when I dream your breasts arrive
before you do and I am a stranger
opening a door between all this talk
and trying to figure each other out
and explain what gets in the way
when I feel no need to explain how it feels
or why the bed is full of rage
and slants to the floor,
or the lamp on the nightstand
tilts in darkness. I'll tell you how it feels.
It feels like believing in nothing
when all I had to give was myself
which you didn't believe was all there
but I gave it anyway regardless of your fear
and yes, I was never all there,
because I don't feel like I know who you are,
because I can't commit myself to another life
when all you think about is not having
and never getting what you want.
No, there's no need to explain
the way my head feels today.
I know that there's a king hiding in the ruins
along the river, and I can picture my body
at the foot of the falls floating
with the tin cans and scraps of wood,
floating for a few minutes of pleasure
in a life of turbulent foam.

Great Falls

DEAR WALT

I'd like to see you right now
walking through Paterson,
through the city Hamilton invented,
birthplace of the sweatshop
and the steam locomotive,
the expression on your face
changing from a look of wonder and awe
as you head down Market Street
waving to strangers.
I'd drive you down
the New Jersey Turnpike
over to Camden
to show you the rest area
named in your honor.
Or, I'd take you out to Long Island
to the shopping mall that bears your name
to show you what America
really thinks of you.
You would see how useless
and reckless we've become.
I imagine you on the street
examining a piece of plastic.
Does it belong to the earth?
It has nothing to return to.
It will not feed the grass.

Queensboro Bridge

DRIVING THROUGH PATERSON

for Maria Gillan

I love this city
and all its constant trouble.
No one bothers me
or bothers to look at it the way I do.
I am happy here
even though I cannot write
about the way I feel.
I never grow tired of these streets
or the narrow rows of houses,
or the old faces of immigrants
peering through faded curtains
in the afternoon.
I love the river and all its rusted bridges.
No one sings of the vacant lots
covered in chicory, or the winos
lined up outside the Evergreen Liquor Store,
or the big-breasted Hispanic who dances
all night naked in The Doctor's Cave Topless Disco.
It is summer and the city is buried in ozone
and goes on with its business.
I turn at an abandoned factory
and past the mills,
driving out alone up Garret Mountain
along the road that takes me to Route 80.
The houses behind me disappear
into a coast of rooftops,
in a landscape of trembling daylight.

Laundromat, Paterson

ROUTE 80

I have had to wait all my life to learn the simplest things.
I have had to learn how to navigate between my dreams
and what I wake to driving out alone along Route 80
to an unwashed city in the rain.
I have had to learn not to burn out like a moth against the glass,
knowing how my father got his Prussian anger from his father,
or how not to suffer loss, that I would fall like my mother
into grim sadness.

And strange that I would even think of her after all these years,
the earth smell from the Hackensack Meadowlands
bringing me back to her dark eyes and long black hair
that autumn we smelled the rain mixing with the rotting reeds,
the first woman I would love--half French, half Vietnamese,
who left me for a soccer player from Brazil.
We parted one spring in Iowa. I remember
driving Route 80 all the way from Indiana seven hours
through Des Moines to get to that mid-western college town,
because I wanted to kill her and disappear; because she was
going to make her life, which was only just beginning,
in Rio de Janeiro.

And as I pull out from behind a semi-trailer and speed up,
I wonder what became of her, thinking she may not even be alive
as I head to work this morning under a low gray sky,
between the wiper's intermittent strokes,
the road disappears slogging with the mist of slow trucks
as I tune a station on the radio,
between the rising octaves of the cellos and the violins,
their heavenly pull of sounds
that feel more like fields of clouds
than a distant continent of firm land.

Pulaski Skyway, Hackensack Meadowlands

ROUTE 46

How long it takes
to drive past the hourly motel
room I remember renting
for a night to escape
for a few hours of sex,
heading west to Lake Hopatcong,
and how the sky gradually closes
as the clouds move in
and a slow, steady rain begins.
I know I grow tired of all these angels,
their lofty absence from this world,
as they swoop down from their billboards
with their long faces and flowing hair,
when I think of how everything disappears,
even the fruit and vegetable stands
that used to sell melons and corn
from the side of the road,
when I remember riding with my brother
on the back seat of the old Ford,
my father behind the wheel,
my mother telling him to pull over
to a diner, for we were tired
from the heat and the long ride
along the Delaware:
the faded brown seats sticky
from popsicles and ice cream.
I know I will never grow tired
of the crumbling concrete overpasses
arching like ancient Roman aqueducts,
or the shredded truck retreads
splayed like alligator pelts
on every shoulder,
or the all-night diners
rising like stainless steel ziggurats
out of the baking asphalt,
or the waitresses as they smile
and lower their heavy breasts
above my face,
or the repeated thud
of the car tires
on the wide cracks
of the cement roadbed
like train tracks
rocking us to sleep.

Motel

Woolworth's

    for Greg Fallon

A kid yells "Mother Fucker" out the school bus window.
I don't think anyone notices the afternoon clouds turning pink along the horizon,
sunlight dripping down the stone facades,
the ancient names of old stores fading like the last century
above the street, above the Spandex women who adjust their prize buttocks,
sweating in the sun as I wonder how this city that has no more memory of itself
than a river has of rain, survives.

Is it just a matter of time, or that peasant woman
who tugs my sleeve demanding "peseta" from every passing stranger:

I can still smell the hotdog counter and the pretzel carousel.
I loved the sound of birds as I entered, the watery bubbles
from aquarium filters over by the plants.
If I imagined like a child walking with my mother,
the store part rainforest, and closed my eyes
I was in some tropical country:
that feathered blue against the orange of forgotten sunsets
after the rain-washed streets erased the footprints
of tired mothers who waited in line
under the red and gold awning
to cash their welfare checks.

And maybe we're all feeling the same rage,
seeing the up-turned fish tanks stacked against the parakeet cages,
sunlight catching on the twisted wire between the shabbiness
of an emptied storefront, rays of sunlight poking in
to finger the dusty hollowness of barren shelves.
Or maybe it's the cheap Plexiglas above the Chinese lettering
or the sound of car alarms and sirens blaring us back.
The city dead in me as I sway down these aisles,
like everything else that fell from my life.

I exit and walk down Main Street
trying to regain my balance
behind the men who walk home
from sweaty jobs with clenched fists
and the women who follow them
pulling their children
like dogs in the rain.

Chinatown

Diner

Here by the cigarette machine the coffee cup I drink from is circa 1950s round,
although the coffee tastes bitter to me now;
and I'm moved to tears because the Formica is cracked
and reminds me of the blue veins running down my mother's legs.

And the tin ashtrays are stacked and bent inside each other next to ketchup bottles
lined up like pints of blood. There's a universe of light in the chrome reflection off
napkin dispensers, a huddled world of comfort in salt & pepper shakers,
sugar slanted like beach-white sand, a stainless steel milk container that is never full.

Grease splatter and sizzle at 2 a.m. remind me
that it is always better here behind the plate glass
in the light than outside traveling through the darkness.

The waitress hits the cash register,
bangs open the drawer
and wets her fingers to count out dollar bills.

Bendix Diner

Cellar Door

AFTERIMAGES

My fascination with urban landscapes grew from living in artist housing in the converted Essex Mill in the historic mill district in Paterson near the Great Falls when they first opened and I moved there in 1984. My windows faced the "Valley of the Rocks," or the cliffs that make up the Great Falls. I could see a ten-acre site of ruined mills and smokestacks on the river. One of the foundations that was still standing was the original 1836 Colt Mill where Samuel Colt manufactured his first revolver--the Paterson Colt. I kept a camera mounted on a tripod and I would take photographs of these ruins at different times, and in different weather. The homeless made their camp sites along the river and at night I could see their camp fires burning. A French friend of mine when he stepped into my loft for the first time said, "C'est la vue d'enfer mais a pas y etre"—like seeing hell without being there.

Deep down, I am drawn to the hulking mill structures that are remnants of an industrial past. There is something more desolate and ominous in an urban wasteland than there is in the vastness of the desert. I love this quality, this combination of beauty amid the ruins of time that I find all around me in a city like Paterson.

Around that same time, a friend gave me a book of George Tice's large format black and white photographs titled *Paterson*. I was taken with their clarity and their austere beauty. Twenty years later I was able to meet George Tice and I helped him scout new locations to shoot for his sequel book titled *Paterson II*. He taught me a great deal about what goes into making a black and white photograph. His work inspired mine and I shared his interest in many of the same subjects. I pay homage to him in several of my photographs.

I was also getting to know the poet Gerald Stern back then. I had just published a long interview with him in the *American Book Review* in 1984. His work had an influence on my writing, and his books at that time, *Lucky Life* and *The Red Coal*, were like George Tice's photographs in that they dealt with things that were overlooked, or that time forgot. His voice resonated with what I was trying to capture.

For me light contains time, and time has a way of entering the very substance of the things that make up this world, and so what I notice has a lot to do with how light illuminates the world around me. It evokes time and the feelings that are associated with its passing. This quality of light is what draws me to photograph certain objects like a spool of white silk left in an abandoned mill, or the way sunlight slants across factory windows to expose the texture in the brick and the dust covering the glass.

S.U.M. Sign Great Falls

School No. 5

Royle Mill

Scrap Iron

Spruce Street

Factory Wall

Milkweed

Figure Painting Window (homage to George Tice)

Mark Hillringhouse is a published poet, essayist, and photographer whose works have been widely exhibited in area galleries. His photography and writing have been published in *The American Poetry Review, The Literary Review, The Paterson Literary Review, The New York Times, The New Jersey Monthly, The Paris Review*, and in many other journals, books, anthologies and magazines. He was the founding editor of *The American Book Review*, and a contributing editor for *The New York Arts Journal*. Thrice nominated for a Pushcart Prize, he is also a three-time recipient of a New Jersey State Council of the Arts Fellowship in Poetry. He has an MFA in creative writing from Fairleigh Dickinson University, and he is a member of the English Department at Passaic County Community College. Visit his photography Website: http://mhillringhouse.zenfolio.com

Acknowledgements

I am grateful to the following anthologies, journals, magazines and book publications in which many of these poems and photographs first appeared:

The American Poetry Review, Blade, Columbia, Coffee House Press, Connecticut River Review, Exit 13, Hanging Loose, Joe Soap's Canoe, Journal of New Jersey Poets, Kshanti, Lips, Long Shot, Mag City, New American Press, New York Arts Journal, Paris Review, Passages North, Paterson Literary Review, Poetry Flash, Redbridge Review, Rutgers University Press, Talisman, Tangerine, The Little Magazine, The World, and *U.S. 1 Worksheet*s

I am also grateful to the following galleries and museums in which several of these photographs were exhibited:

Paterson Museum (group show) 2003

Hamilton Club Gallery, Passaic County Community College,

exhibition titled: "Parts of a World" 2004

Main Street Gallery, Groton, NY Juried Photography Exhibition 2005

Warner Gallery, Millbrook, NY 2006

Paterson Museum "Visual Art by Writers" 2006

First Annual Great Falls Art Show, Paterson Museum, 2008

Salmagundi Art Club's Annual Juried Photography Competition, New York, NY 2009

Ben Shahn Gallery, William Paterson University, 2009

Cheng Library, William Paterson University, 2010

Cheng Library, Urban Paterson Photography Exhibition, 2011

Broadway Gallery, Passaic County Community College, retrospective exhibition: "Paterson in Color and Black & White, 2011

In addition, my photograph "Great Falls, Paterson" won honorable mention and publication in the National Parks Natural Landmarks 2012 Calendar, and my poem "Orpheus" won the 2011 Allen Ginsberg Poetry Prize.

I would like to thank the New Jersey State Council on the Arts for their generous support for fellowships in 1985, 1989, and 1998.

www.ingramcontent.com/pod-product-compliance
Lightning Source LLC
Chambersburg PA
CBHW042024150426
43198CB00002B/57